LET'S LEARN
MINI-BOOKS
Our Nation

by Kathleen M. Hollenbeck

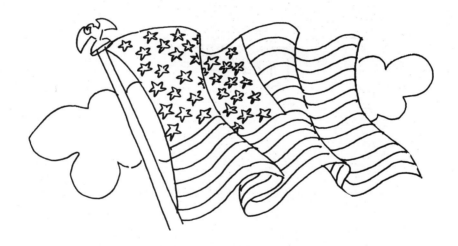

S C H O L A S T I C
PROFESSIONAL BOOKS

New York • Toronto • London • Auckland • Sydney • Mexico City
New Delhi • Hong Kong • Buenos Aires

To all those who bravely served our nation
during and beyond the tragedy of September 11, 2001

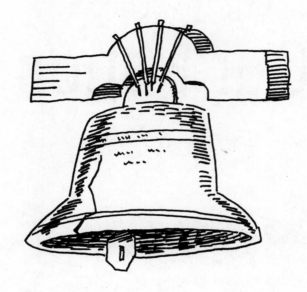

Cover design by **Sydney Wright**
Cover and interior artwork by **George Ulrich**
Interior design by **Holly Grundon**

ISBN: 0-439-32331-2
Copyright © 2003 by Kathleen M. Hollenbeck
All rights reserved. Published by Scholastic Inc.
Printed in the U.S.A.

5 6 7 8 9 10   40   09 08 07 06 05

Contents

Introduction

As adults, we know what it means to be a United States citizen. We understand the privileges and opportunities it affords. We appreciate the significance of the Statue of Liberty, the beauty of the Liberty Bell's first toll, and the magnificence found in fluttering banners of red, white, and blue. These are symbols of our country. They are symbols of freedom, strength, and courage that inspire citizens of our nation to stand up and proudly say, "I am an American."

Children sometimes have difficulty understanding the patriotic symbols and the workings of democracy. *Let's Learn Mini-Books: Our Nation* is designed to deepen your students' grasp of our country's ideals and the beliefs for which our nation stands. As students learn the history and meaning behind some of our country's most visible symbols, they will feel a deeper alliance with the forebears of our nation, whose primary hopes and dreams centered on establishing a country of freedom, ruled by democracy and open to all. As children learn the workings of our government, they will understand how democracy affects lives—and what it takes to secure and maintain justice. Our patriotic songs can take on new meaning as they evolve from memorized verse into treasured declarations of history, passion, and pride.

—Kathleen M. Hollenbeck

Background Information and Activities
for Use With the Mini-Books

Our 50 States

PAGE 21

The United States is the world's third largest country in population and the fourth largest in area. Delaware, the first state, was established in 1787. Hawaii, the fiftieth, was established in 1959.

★ **Make a State Word Wall.** On a large sheet of butcher paper, outline the shape of your state, and invite students to write inside it the names of people, places, and things that they feel represent their state.

★ **Design Board Games.** Let students work in groups, each choosing one state and designing a board game that will teach others about it. Encourage students to research thoroughly and base their games on solid facts.

★ **Track State Teams.** Select a sport that is in season and ask each student to choose a team to follow from 1 of the 50 states. For several weeks, have students use newspapers to track their team's performance. Graph the results.

BOOKS TO SHARE

Leedy, Loreen. ***Celebrate the 50 States!*** (Holiday House, 1999). This colorful, upbeat tribute to our country is packed with state facts and details. Have students use it to write challenging questions for classmates to answer.

Stienecker, David L. ***First Facts About the States*** (Blackbirch Press, 1996). This photographic resource highlights each of the 50 states.

Stars and Stripes Forever!

Stars and Stripes Forever!

PAGE 23

Some historians believe Betsy Ross sewed one of the first American flags in the late 1700s, based on a design shown to her by George Washington. The flag's stars represent the heavens and people's belief in a God. The stripes symbolize rays of light radiating from the sun.

★ **Design Your Own Flag.** Invite your students to design and draw a flag that represents them—hobbies they enjoy, colors they prefer, and so on.

★ **Flags Across the Country.** Ask students to choose one state and study its flag. Have them draw the flag and explain what its symbols mean.

★ **Respect the Flag.** Review traditional guidelines for handling the U.S. flag. For example, explain that the flag should never touch the ground, and it must be lowered at sunset unless a light shines on it.

BOOKS TO SHARE

Herman, John. *Red, White, and Blue: The Story of the American Flag* (Grosset & Dunlap, 1998). This early reader details the history and evolution of the American flag, from its revolutionary beginning to its current 50 stars.

The Bald Eagle

The Bald Eagle

PAGE 25

After six years of debate, the bald eagle was selected as our national bird in 1782. Considering the bird a symbol of courage, strength, and freedom, early U.S. leaders chose the bald eagle over an alternate choice, the wild turkey.

★ **Vote for a Symbol.** Elect a class animal. Invite students to select two or three animals that symbolize your class in character, size, or another way. Hold a debate if necessary. Encourage students to defend their choices and identify reasons why their animal of choice would be most fitting.

- ★ **Adjectives of Honor.** Invite students to come up with synonyms for the words that describe our national bird, such as courage, freedom, and strength. Urge them to think of additional words that describe our nation and its qualities.

- ★ **Design a Family Crest.** Have students create their own family crest and tell the class what its symbols mean. Compare the family symbols with the Great Seal of the United States, the symbol of a nation.

BOOKS TO SHARE

Quiri, Patricia Ryon. *The Bald Eagle* (Children's Press, 1998). The author explores the behavior and characteristics of this American symbol.

Let Freedom Ring!

Originally cast in England, the Liberty Bell first hung in Philadelphia's Independence Hall in 1753. The bell is famous for its symbolism of American freedom and for the crack along its side.

Let Freedom Ring!

PAGE 27

- ★ **What Does Freedom Mean to Me?** Using construction paper, draw and cut out the silhouette of the Liberty Bell. Give each student a bell and ask him or her to write on it a sentence that tells what freedom means. Post the bells on a bulletin board display entitled "America, Home of the Free."

- ★ **Which Symbol Is It?** As students gather knowledge of the Liberty Bell and other U.S. symbols, invite them to write riddles about them. Classmates can read the riddles and rely on clues to identify the symbols.

- ★ **Ring Out the Bells!** Emphasize the importance of bells as a means of communication. Brainstorm various reasons why people ring bells: to announce good news, to see if someone is home, to indicate the start of a school period, and so on. Help students list the many different kinds of bells people use in their community, from those found in churches to elevators.

BOOKS TO SHARE

Wilson, Jon. *The Liberty Bell: The Sounds of Freedom* (The Child's World, Inc., 1999). This book describes how the Liberty Bell rang out its first call for freedom in 1776.

The Statue of Liberty

PAGE 29

The Statue of Liberty is one of the tallest statues in the world. Historians say that the sculptor, Frédéric-Auguste Bartholdi, used his mother as the model for the statue's face and his wife as the model for the arms.

⭐ **How Big Is She Really?** Working in teams, have students measure and multiply real-life objects or locations (yardsticks, tables, school hallways) to grasp the actual size of the Statue of Liberty. Measurements students might explore include the height of the statue (151 feet, 1 inch), the width of the mouth (3 feet), the size of one fingernail (13 by 10 inches), and the length of the nose (4 feet, 6 inches). They might also calculate how long it would take to climb the 171 steps inside the statue.

⭐ **Share Bartholdi's Vision.** The sculptor who created the Statue of Liberty plotted every inch of her on paper before using copper and steel to build her. Have your students create blueprints for statues of their own. Encourage them to be creative, giving their statues a name and telling what the statues represent.

BOOKS TO SHARE

Bunting, Eve. *A Picnic in October* (Harcourt Brace & Company, 1999). This is a touching, realistic story of a family's annual trip to Ellis Island.

Curlee, Lynn. *Liberty* (Atheneum Books for Young Readers, 2000). Lady Liberty comes together piece by piece in this dramatic picture book.

Who Is Uncle Sam?

PAGE 31

Congress officially recognizes the inspiration for the symbol "Uncle Sam" as being a New York businessman named Sam Wilson. Wilson supplied the U.S. Army with beef during the War of 1812. Experts believe soldiers first called Sam Wilson—and then the United States—Uncle Sam.

★ **Share a Poem.**

> **Who Is Uncle Sam?**
> Do you know who I am? My name is Uncle Sam.
> I wear red, white, and blue. I wear a top hat, too!
> I'm like the flag, you see. I stand for liberty.
> United States, I am. My name is Uncle Sam.

★ **Write a Message From Uncle Sam.** What message would Uncle Sam give U.S. citizens today? Have students design their own posters with a message they feel Americans need to hear.

★ **Draw Patriotic Cartoons.** Put students in the illustrator's chair. Have them draw cartoons about America, featuring Uncle Sam or famous Americans.

BOOKS TO SHARE

West, Delno C. *Uncle Sam and Old Glory* (Atheneum Books for Young Readers, 2000). This book explores the origin and meaning of 15 symbols that embody freedom, courage, and democracy.

Who Leads Our Nation?

The democratic system ensures that no one person or branch of government holds exclusive power. Democracy allows Americans the freedom to live as they choose as long as they respect and abide by the laws of our nation.

Who Leads Our Nation?

PAGE 33

★ **We Are the U.S. Government.** Divide the class into three groups. Ask each group to assume the identity of one branch of government: legislative, executive, or judicial. Have students learn about the jobs their branch carries out. Then have them role-play to demonstrate these jobs.

★ **Which Branch Is It?** Have students make up riddles about the branches of government and read them aloud while classmates guess which branch they're describing. For example, a riddle might read: "When people disagree or fight, my branch of government sets things right. We know just what the law's about. We help people to work things out."

BOOKS TO SHARE

St. George, Judith. *So You Want to Be President* (Philomel Books, 2000). This Caldecott winner informs and entertains, examining the presidency in every which way.

Sobel, Syl. *How the U.S. Government Works* (Barron's Educational Series, 1999). The author skillfully explains a difficult concept in terms young readers can understand.

Washington, D.C.:
Our Nation's Capital

PAGE
35

Washington, D.C.: Our Nation's Capital

In 1800, headquarters for our national government moved from Philadelphia, Pennsylvania, to Washington, D.C. George Washington chose the District of Columbia so that no state would have ownership of the capital city.

⭐ **Postcards From the Capital.** Turn blank index cards into postcards—from Washington, D.C.! On one side, ask students to draw a picture of a famous building or landmark in the capital city. On the other side, have them write a note to a friend, telling what they saw when they "visited" there.

⭐ **A Capital Quilt.** Hand out construction paper in various colors. Have each student draw a landmark she or he would see in Washington, D.C., such as the White House or the Lincoln Memorial. Connect the papers to make a colorful quilt of our nation's capital.

⭐ **Plan a Tour.** Obtain tour books for Washington, D.C., from its chamber of commerce. Let children browse through them and work in groups to plan a three-day itinerary showing what they would do while visiting the city.

BOOKS TO SHARE

Fradin, Dennis Brindell. *Washington, D.C.* (Children's Press, 1992). The author presents a detailed view of our nation's capital.

Stein, R. Conrad. *Washington, D.C.* (Children's Press, 1999). This resource book provides a wealth of information about Washington, D.C.

What Is the White House?

The White House has been home to every U.S. president except George Washington. Built in 1800, the building has been renovated many times for repair and improvement, the most notable time being after British soldiers burned it down in 1814.

PAGE 37

⭐ **Make a White House Show.** Give each student an 18-inch strip of adding machine paper. Have children draw lines to divide the strip into 3-inch sections. Then in each section have them draw a scene from the White House, such as the Oval Office or the Blue Room. Students can then roll up the paper and unroll it as they give their own moving tour of the White House.

⭐ **What Really Happened?** Over the years, presidents and their families have used the White House in various ways. Provide resource books and have students work in teams to find and illustrate something they find unique, humorous, or unusual that happened in the White House. For example, what is now the formal East Room was once home to Tad Lincoln's pet goat.

BOOKS TO SHARE

Sorensen, Lynda. **The White House** (The Rourke Book Company, 1994). A colorful, simply written view of the White House both long ago and today.

Thomsen, Steven. **The White House** (Capstone Press, 1991). The author describes the history and architecture of the White House.

Order in the Supreme Court

The Supreme Court is open from October through June. Supreme Court justices work in two-week intervals. For two weeks, they listen to cases. For the next two weeks, they discuss what they have heard. Of the 5,000 requests presented each year, about 200 cases go before the Supreme Court.

PAGE 39

⭐ **Right to Trial by Jury.** Talk with your students about the Bill of Rights amendment which ensures U.S. citizens the right to a trial by a jury of peers. Explain what it entails, and invite students to share their opinions. Why is this right so important?

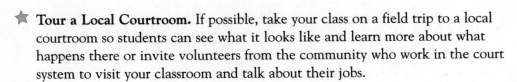

★ **Tour a Local Courtroom.** If possible, take your class on a field trip to a local courtroom so students can see what it looks like and learn more about what happens there or invite volunteers from the community who work in the court system to visit your classroom and talk about their jobs.

★ **Which Cases Get to the Supreme Court?** As a class, briefly research and discuss some of the most famous court cases decided by the Supreme Court.

BOOKS TO SHARE — Sanders, Mark. *The Supreme Court* (Steadwell Books, 2000). This factual book describes the purpose and workings of the nation's top court, highlighting significant court cases and notable justices.

What Happens in the Capitol Building?

PAGE 41

What Happens in the Capitol Building?

The U.S. Capitol sits on Capitol Hill, the hub of government in Washington, D.C. It has been home to the Senate and the House of Representatives since 1800. The Capitol holds many mementos of American history and has been the site of funerals for famous Americans, such as Abraham Lincoln and John F. Kennedy.

★ **Check Out Webquest.** Take your students online to complete the United States Symbols Webquest, a prepared list of questions about U.S. symbols. The web site is: **http://www.nashville.k12.tn.us/webquests/united_states_symbols.htm**

★ **Know Who's Who in Government.** Ask students to scan local newspapers to find pictures of their state representatives in the Senate and the House of Representatives. Post pictures of these men and women in the classroom.

BOOKS TO SHARE — Van Wie, Nancy Ann. *Travels with Max: The U.S. Capitol Building* (Max's Publications, 1998). This fun, informative book explains the history of the United States and the workings of our government.

This Is My State

This Is My State

PAGE 43

Each state in the nation has its own symbols, landmarks, and characteristics. Immerse your students in a study of their own state—from its early settlement to present-day events.

⭐ **Write a State Flip-Book.** Ask students to place five sheets of paper in a stack and staple at the top. On the top sheet, have children draw a line four inches from the bottom and then cut off the paper below that line. On the second sheet, have students measure three inches from the bottom and cut off the paper below that line. Continue in this manner. On the top page, invite children to draw the shape of their state and details that make it unique. Have them label the underlying pages with the names of their state symbols (state flag, state bird, and so on) and draw them.

⭐ **Read Across America.** As a class, find one fiction book set in each state of the union! Write the name of each book on paper and pin it to a U.S. map.

BOOKS TO SHARE

For informative, fact-filled books on individual states, check out these series for ages 4–8: **Checkerboard Geography: The United States** (Abdo & Daughters, 1998); and **The States and Their Symbols** (Hilltop Books, 2000).

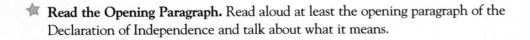

What Is the Declaration of Independence?

What Is the Declaration of Independence?

PAGE 45

Two days after voting to declare independence from Great Britain, delegates from 12 of the 13 colonies met in Philadelphia, Pennsylvania, to sign the Declaration of Independence. Thomas Jefferson wrote the bulk of the Declaration. He was helped by Ben Franklin, John Adams, Roger Sherman, and Robert Livingston.

⭐ **Read the Opening Paragraph.** Read aloud at least the opening paragraph of the Declaration of Independence and talk about what it means.

⭐ **Make Biography Trading Cards.** Have each student draw the picture of a famous American, such as Ben Franklin, on a blank (3-by 5-inch) index card. On the back, ask students to write information about that person and draw one object that the person would have treasured in his or her lifetime. Invite students to trade cards with each other.

BOOKS TO SHARE

Freedman, Russell. *Give Me Liberty! The Story of the Declaration of Independence* (Holiday House, 2000). The author looks at the revolutionary period from the Boston Tea Party to the Declaration of Independence.

What Does the Constitution Mean to Me?

What Does the Constitution Mean to Me?

PAGE 47

The Founding Fathers signed the U.S. Constitution on September 17, 1787. It was ratified by all 13 states by May of 1790. In 1791, Congress added the Bill of Rights, an amendment describing the rights that all U.S. citizens possess as human beings, such as freedom of speech and religion.

⭐ **What Right Means the Most?** Review the items outlined in the Bill of Rights. On crinkled parchment paper, have students use black marker to write about an American right they enjoy.

⭐ **Write a Classroom Constitution.** Take the classroom rules your students already follow and have students write them up formally in a classroom constitution. Add new rules if necessary. Be sure students vote to ratify the document!

BOOKS TO SHARE

Fritz, Jean. *Shh! We're Writing the Constitution* (G.P. Putnam's Sons, 1987). Fritz's style is user-friendly, and young readers will delight in her presentation of our nation's first legislators.

Prolman, Marilyn. *The Story of the Constitution* (Children's Press, 1969). The author talks about how the states joined to form one central governing body that still works well today.

The Pledge of Allegiance

The Pledge of Allegiance

PAGE 49

In 1888, the children's magazine *The Youth's Companion* published an article asking children to donate pennies to help buy American flags for schools across the nation. In response, American schoolchildren contributed enough pennies to purchase 30,000 flags. That same year, two employees of the magazine, Francis Bellamy and James Upham, began to plan a school celebration that became what is known today as Columbus Day.

⭐ **Write a Pledge.** Encourage students to determine what they would like to do to help, support, or honor their country. Have them write their own pledges to the United States.

⭐ **Understand the Pledge.** Write the words to the pledge on tag-board strips and place them in a pocket chart. As a class, replace words in the pledge with synonyms to help clarify their meaning and students' understanding of the pledge itself. For example, "I pledge allegiance" might be replaced with "I promise to love and be faithful to my country."

BOOKS TO SHARE

The Pledge of Allegiance (Scholastic Inc., 2001). A photographic tribute to our nation's flag and to the freedom and spirit it represents.

Swanson, June. *I Pledge Allegiance* (Carolrhoda Books, 1990). The author describes how reciting the pledge came to be part of the school-day routine.

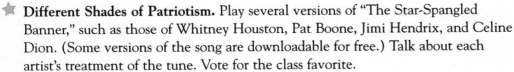

The Star-Spangled Banner

The Star-Spangled Banner

PAGE 51

Francis Scott Key wrote "The Star-Spangled Banner" on the back of an envelope the morning after the British attack on Baltimore's Fort McHenry during the War of 1812. Congress appointed it our national anthem in 1931.

⭐ **Different Shades of Patriotism.** Play several versions of "The Star-Spangled Banner," such as those of Whitney Houston, Pat Boone, Jimi Hendrix, and Celine Dion. (Some versions of the song are downloadable for free.) Talk about each artist's treatment of the tune. Vote for the class favorite.

★ **Explore Emotion.** How do you feel inside when you hear "The Star-Spangled Banner"? What is it that inspires respect and awe? Discuss this with your students. Invite them to tell why it is important for a country to have an anthem. Talk about times when our national anthem has moved people to tears (at the Olympics, for example) and why this might happen.

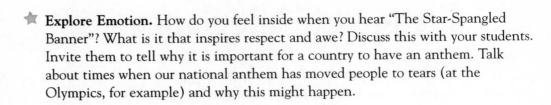

BOOKS TO SHARE

Kroll, Steven. ***By the Dawn's Early Light: The Story of the Star-Spangled Banner*** (Scholastic, 1994). The story of how Francis Scott Key, moved by the sight of the American flag still standing after battle, penned the now-famous poem.

St. Pierre, Stephanie. ***Our National Anthem*** (The Millbrook Press, 1992). The history and importance of the Star-Spangled Banner receive full attention in this informative account of our national song.

PAGE 53

America the Beautiful

Katharine Lee Bates wrote "America the Beautiful" in 1893. Historians say her inspiration came from a view she had seen from Pikes Peak in Colorado. First published in a magazine, *The Congregationalist*, in 1895, the poem was later set to music by American composer Samuel Augustus Ward.

★ **I Am the United States.** Have students write a song, poem, or story in which the United States speaks. As America, students can talk about the country's natural beauty, the strength and courage of its people, the changes it has undergone as a result of growth, time, and technology, and so on.

★ **Sing About America!** Share other patriotic songs with your students. Favorites include "Yankee Doodle," "Battle Hymn of the Republic," "God Bless America," and "America."

BOOKS TO SHARE

Guthrie, Woody. ***This Land Is Your Land*** (Little, Brown, 1998). A beloved folk song springs to life through intricate folk-style paintings that take readers across the country, showing various portraits of America.

The Fourth of July

The first Fourth of July celebration took place in 1777 in Philadelphia, Pennsylvania. Residents placed lighted candles in the windows of their homes to honor the first year of American independence from Great Britain.

PAGE
55

- **We Celebrate the Fourth.** Have students draw pictures to show how they and their families celebrate the Fourth of July. Place the pictures inside starburst-shaped frames cut from colorful paper. Hang them for display.

- **Happy Birthday, America!** Challenge students to calculate the age of the United States, based on the nation declaring its independence in 1776.

- **Make Shoe-Box Floats.** Hold a mini-parade in your classroom—with patriotic floats made from shoe boxes. Provide red, white, and blue paint, paper, ribbons, adhesive stars, and toothpick flags.

BOOKS TO SHARE

Gore, Willma Willis. *Independence Day* (Enslow Publishers, Inc., 1993). The author describes the history and symbolism of our nation's birthday.

Martin Luther King, Jr., Day

Dr. Martin Luther King, Jr., won the Nobel Peace Prize for his nonviolent protest of segregation. His efforts did much to advance equal and fair treatment for all people in this country. Each year, on the third Monday in January, American citizens celebrate Dr. Martin Luther King's life and achievements.

PAGE
57

- **Martin's Dream.** After reading books to learn more about Martin Luther King, Jr., ask students to draw a picture of the famous American with a dream bubble over his head. In the bubble, have students illustrate some aspect of Dr. King's dream for African Americans.

Peace Prevails. Martin Luther King, Jr., believed in using peaceful means to protest unfair conditions. Talk with your students about peaceful ways in which people can enact change, such as by leading marches, making speeches, and distributing flyers. Divide the class into groups. Have each group demonstrate a peaceful protest to an unfair situation that is real or fictitious.

BOOKS TO SHARE

Sorensen, Lynda. *Martin Luther King Jr. Day* (The Rourke Press, Inc., 1994). The author's tale of how we celebrate the birthday of a famous African American whose contributions toward our nation were unparalleled in his time.

Presidents' Day

Presidents' Day

PAGE 59

On Presidents' Day, our nation honors two of America's greatest presidents, George Washington and Abraham Lincoln.

★ **Line Up the Presidents.** Make a presidential procession—with lunch bags! Have students decorate lunch bags to represent U.S. presidents. (Be sure they draw the head on the closed end.) Stuff the bags with newspaper and stand them upright, heads up.

★ **Whose Face Is That?** Help students identify the names and faces of the U.S. presidents featured on U.S. coins, dollar bills, and monuments such as Mount Rushmore. Talk briefly about what made these presidents stand out in the hearts of Americans.

BOOKS TO SHARE

Ansary, Mir Tamim. *Presidents' Day* (Heinemann Library, 1999). The author explains the origin of both the presidency and Presidents' Day in this simply written, highly visual book for young readers.

Memorial Day

Memorial Day began as Decoration Day, a time set aside to decorate the graves of soldiers who died in the Civil War. Over the years, it was changed to honor soldiers who died in all American wars.

Memorial Day

PAGE
61

⭐ **Local Celebrations.** What does your students' community do to celebrate Memorial Day? Call the town hall or chamber of commerce to find out, and talk about it with your students.

⭐ **Patriotic Ribbons.** Invite students to remember loved ones who are living. Cut white prize ribbons from tag board. Have children use crayons, stickers, glitter, and other craft items in red, white, and blue to make patriotic prize ribbons for people who truly make a difference in their lives. Be sure each student writes a brief sentence or two explaining the award.

BOOKS TO SHARE

Sorensen, Lynda. **Memorial Day** (The Rourke Press, 1994). In photographs and prose, the author describes the meaning of Memorial Day.

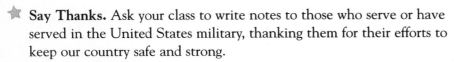

Veterans Day

Veterans Day, once called Armistice Day, was originally a time set aside to remember soldiers who died in World War I. After the Korean war, the holiday was renamed and designated as a day to thank all men and women who have served in the armed forces during wartime or peacetime.

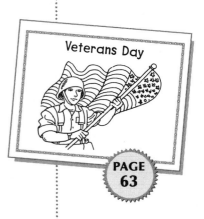

Veterans Day

PAGE
63

⭐ **Say Thanks.** Ask your class to write notes to those who serve or have served in the United States military, thanking them for their efforts to keep our country safe and strong.

BOOKS TO SHARE

Sorensen, Lynda. **Veterans Day** (The Rourke Press, 1994). The author sheds light on the history and significance of this patriotic holiday.

How to Make the Mini-books

E ach mini-book in this resource focuses on a U.S. symbol, landmark, document, holiday, or song. Within each lies an opportunity to awaken the citizens in your students and inspire in them a sense of patriotism they can carry with them for the rest of their lives.

Directions

1. Carefully remove the mini-book to be copied, tearing along the perforation.

2. Make a double-sided copy of the mini-book for each student. If your machine does not have a double-sided function, make copies of the title page A first. (You might want to make extra copies.) Place these copies in the machine's paper tray blank-side up. Then make a test copy of page B to be sure that it copies onto the back of page A. It is important that the mini-book's page 1 copies directly behind the cover page.

3. Once you have a double-sided copy, cut the page in half along the dotted line.

4. Place page B behind page A.

5. Fold the pages in half along the solid line.

6. Check to be sure that the pages are in proper order, then staple them together along the book's spine.

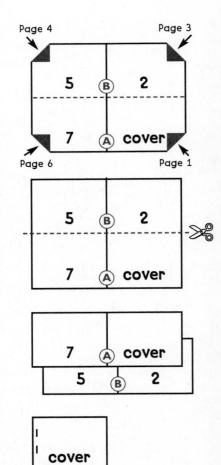

Page 2

All 50 states share one leader, the president of the United States. The president works for the good of all U.S. citizens. Each state has a leader as well. The leader of a state is called a governor.

Ⓑ

Page A

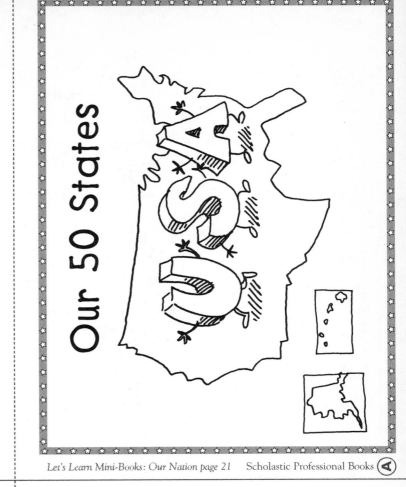

Our 50 States

Page 5

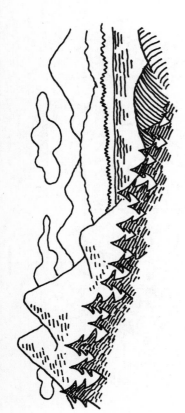

The United States is a land of beauty. From snow-capped mountains to flat, sandy beaches, the land varies across the country. Fields and forests stretch for miles. Canyons, valleys, and lakes can be found from the East Coast to the West.

Page 7

The United States is a land of beauty, freedom, and opportunity. People feel proud to say America is their home. Why do you feel proud to live in the United States?

_____

_____

_____

_____

The United States is a country of freedom. People who live in the United States are free to make their own choices. They can choose their own homes and jobs and churches. They can choose what to read, and they can say what they think and feel.

For hundreds of years, people have come to the United States from other lands. They have come to find freedom, work, and a new way of life. Because America is home to people from all over the world, some people call it a "melting pot."

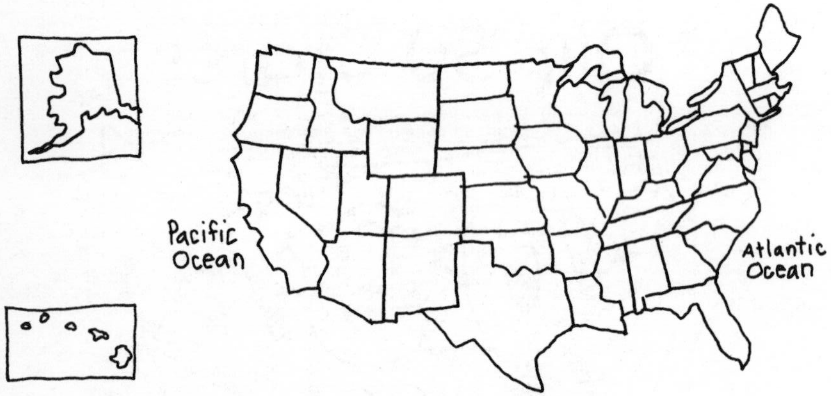

The United States is one of the largest countries in the world. It stretches from the Atlantic Ocean to the Pacific Ocean. Fifty states belong to the United States.

Pacific Ocean

Atlantic Ocean

All across the United States, Americans work hard to keep our nation strong. People use their skills to make planes and roadways. They discover new medicines, build faster computers, and help the poor.

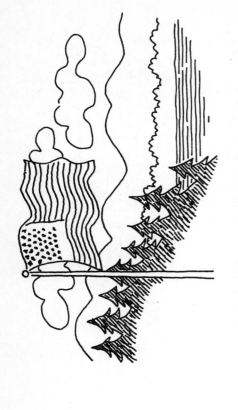

The U.S. flag is red, white, and blue. These colors tell about our country. Red stands for courage. White stands for purity. Blue stands for justice.

Ⓑ

2

Stars and Stripes Forever!

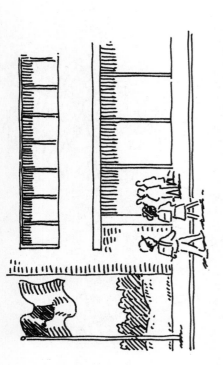

The flag waves all across the United States. We see it on schools, banks, and other government buildings. We see it at airports and all entrances to our country.

5

We look at the flag when we say the Pledge of Allegiance. We promise to be faithful to the United States. We feel proud to live in a country of freedom and justice.

7

1

This is the flag of the United States of America. Some people call it Old Glory. We think of our country when we see the United States flag.

3

The U.S. flag has 13 stripes. They stand for the 13 colonies that first formed our country. The flag also has 50 stars. They stand for the 50 states in the United States today.

4

People fly the flag on special days, such as our country's birthday. They fly it when something sad happens in our nation or to honor people who have died.

6

Some people say Betsy Ross sewed the very first flag. At that time, our country was new. Americans wanted one flag to show they were a unified nation.

Page 2

The bald eagle is not bald at all. It has white feathers on its head and tail. It gets its name from the word *piebald*, which means "marked with white."

Ⓑ

2

Page A (cover)

The Bald Eagle

Page 5

The laws worked. Today there are more than 70,000 bald eagles soaring through the skies. They live only in the United States and other parts of North America.

5

Page 7

Where might you see a picture of our national bird? Look for it on one-dollar bills, quarters, half dollars, and silver dollars. Where else might you see the bald eagle?

7

3

The bald eagle became our national bird in 1782. Our leaders chose the bald eagle because it is a bird of strength, courage, and freedom.

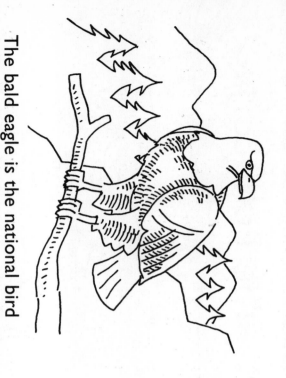

1

The bald eagle is the national bird of the United States. It is an important symbol of our nation.

4

Not long ago, bald eagles were in danger of dying out. Our government made laws to protect them. The laws say that no one can hunt bald eagles. The laws also help stop pollution that is harmful to birds.

6

The bald eagle appears on the presidential flag and on the Great Seal of the United States. The eagle can also be found on one-dollar bills and many U.S. coins.

Let Freedom Ring!

Ⓐ

In 1776, the Liberty Bell rang to celebrate our new nation. America had been made up of colonies that belonged to England. In 1776, the colonies broke free and formed their own country.

Ⓑ

2

The bell holds a special place in the hearts of all Americans. It reminds us of the struggle it took to become a free country.

5

Many people visit the Liberty Bell. They think about our nation's early days. Liberty means freedom. The Liberty Bell is a symbol of our country's freedom.

7

The Liberty Bell rang for other special events, too. It rang to announce important meetings and to celebrate the Fourth of July. In 1846, the bell rang in honor of George Washington's birthday.

The most famous bell in America is called the Liberty Bell. The Liberty Bell hangs in Philadelphia, Pennsylvania. It has been there for more than 200 years.

Today the Liberty Bell does not ring. It cracked long ago. John Pass and Charles Stow melted the bell and made it again. They did this twice. Both bells cracked.

In 1776, the Liberty Bell was moved to a special place called the Liberty Bell Pavilion. Before that, it hung in Independence Hall, where our leaders signed the Declaration of Independence.

The woman is the Statue of Liberty. Some people call her Lady Liberty. Liberty means freedom.

Ⓑ

The Statue of Liberty

The Statue of Liberty is sturdy. She has a strong steel frame inside her body. The Statue of Liberty is enormous. Her thumb is as tall as a grown man. Her right arm is longer than a school bus!

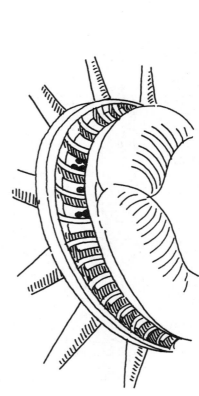

More than 5 million people visit the Statue of Liberty each year. When the statue is open, some people climb 354 steps to stand inside the statue's head and look out on New York Harbor. They feel thankful for the freedom we enjoy.

3

The people of France gave the Statue of Liberty to the United States. They wanted to honor our nation's hundredth birthday and our dream of freedom.

1

A woman stands tall in New York Harbor. She is dressed in robes and holds a torch. The torch stands for the light of freedom that shines for all people.

4

A sculptor named Frédéric-Auguste Bartholdi made the statue. He and his helpers built it in more than 300 pieces. Each part was made separately in France. The pieces were put together in the United States.

6

Lady Liberty wears a crown that has seven spikes. They stand for Earth's seven continents and seven seas. Broken chains lie under her feet. They are the chains of slavery, crushed by freedom.

Uncle Sam is dressed in red, white, and blue. These are the colors of the United States flag. We think of our flag and our country when we see Uncle Sam.

Ⓑ

2

Who Is Uncle Sam?

Uncle Sam has appeared in television cartoons, telling what it means to be an American. He has also been drawn as a superhero, fighting for freedom.

5

Uncle Sam is a symbol of the strength and dedication of our government leaders. Hooray for Uncle Sam!

7

This is a picture of Uncle Sam. He is a cartoon character who stands for the United States government.

1

You might have heard people say, "I'll do it for Uncle Sam!" They mean that they plan to do something to support our country or follow its laws.

3

Sometimes people print Uncle Sam's picture on posters. The most famous one was printed during World War I. It showed Uncle Sam pointing. It said, "I Want You for U.S. Army."

4

Across America, people sell Uncle Sam dolls and statues. His picture is also on mugs, buttons, and other items. People feel patriotic when they see Uncle Sam.

6

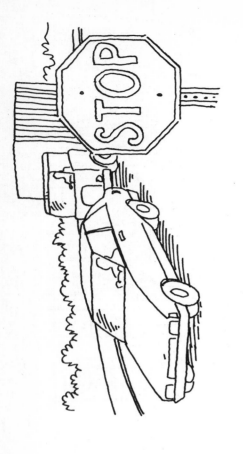

2

The legislative branch is called Congress. Congress makes the laws, or rules, that all U.S. citizens must follow.

Ⓑ

Who Leads Our Nation?

5

The government needs money to do its jobs. It gets money from people who live in the United States. Congress decides how much money the government will need and how it will be spent.

When people choose their leaders, the government is called a democracy. The United States is a democracy. It is run by and for the people of our nation.

7

The executive branch makes sure the laws work and that people obey them. The president is the head of the executive branch.

The United States government has three parts, called branches. They all work together to help the country run smoothly.

The judicial branch interprets the laws, or figures out what they mean. When people disagree about a law, a judge will help them decide what is right.

U.S. citizens have a voice in government. Those who are age 18 or older have the right to vote. They choose the leaders who will make and carry out the laws.

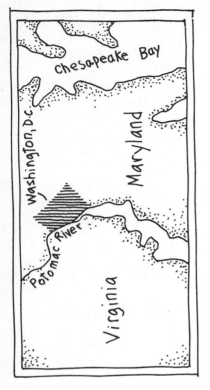

The capital city was named after George Washington. The letters D and C stand for District of Columbia, an area of land that is not owned by any state.

2

B

Washington, D.C.: Our Nation's Capital

A

Exciting things happen in the capital city. Congress makes laws there. Workers print U.S. postage stamps and paper money. Museums display pieces of history, such as the first plane ever to fly.

5

Millions of people visit Washington, D.C., every year. They come to view our country's symbols and enjoy the beauty of our nation's capital.

7

3

Washington, D.C., lies between the states of Maryland and Virginia. The Potomac River runs along the edge of the city.

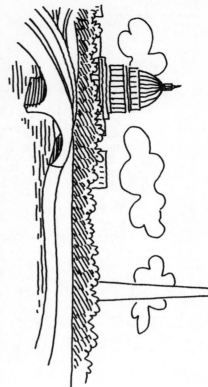

Washington, D.C., is home to many famous buildings. The White House, the U.S. Capitol, and the Washington Monument are just three of the many important ones.

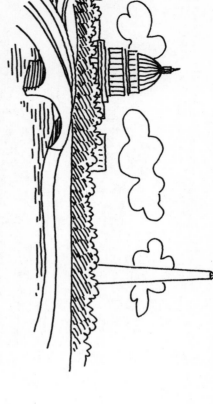

US Capitol

The White House

Washington Monument

4

1

Washington, D.C., is the capital of the United States of America. It is the home of the president and the headquarters of our U.S. government.

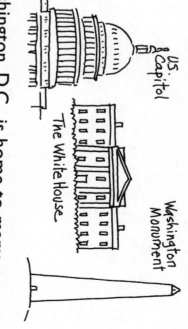

Washington, D.C., is also home to Arlington National Cemetery. It is the resting place of more than 250,000 soldiers who died in American wars.

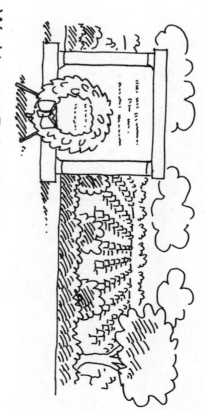

6

George Washington
helped plan the
White House. Workers
began building it in 1792.
In 1800, John Adams was
the first president to move in.

Ⓑ 2

What Is the
White House?

The White House has places for fun, too.
There is a private bowling alley, a movie
theater, and a swimming pool inside the
White House.

5

Millions of visitors come to the White
House each year. Visitors only get to see
a small part of the White House, but they
are touched by its splendor and grace.

7

3

The White House has 132 rooms. Some of these are bedrooms and dining rooms. The president and the president's family sleep, eat, and entertain guests there.

1

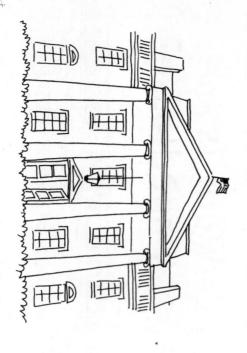

The White House is a famous building in Washington, D.C. The president of the United States lives and works there.

6

U.S. history fills the White House. Many rooms hold furniture, paintings, and dishes bought by early presidents. Even Abraham Lincoln's bed is still there.

4

Some rooms are offices where the president and his staff work. The president signs bills and holds meetings in a special room called the Oval Office.

A court is a body or part, of government that settles disagreements. Courts decide whether people are guilty of crimes and how they should be punished.

Ⓑ

2

Order in the Supreme Court

The Supreme Court holds more power than any other court in the United States. Nine judges sit on the Supreme Court. Together they listen to each court case. They talk about it and decide what to do.

5

Supreme Court justices are chosen by the president and by Congress. Once they are elected, justices may keep their jobs for their whole lifetime.

7

3

Courts also decide what is fair. They study the laws of our country. Sometimes courts change laws to make sure they will work for the good of all Americans.

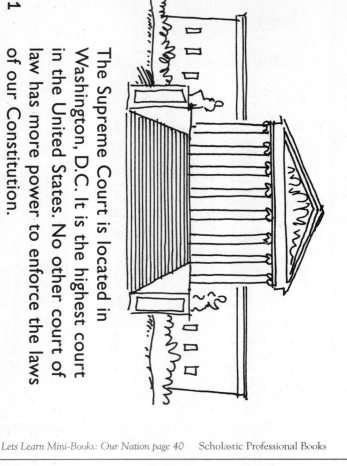

1

The Supreme Court is located in Washington, D.C. It is the highest court in the United States. No other court of law has more power to enforce the laws of our Constitution.

4

Each state has its own courts. Some cities and towns have courts, too. If people do not agree with what state or local courts say, they might ask to take their problems to a more powerful court.

6

Only the most important court cases go before the Supreme Court. Each year, the Supreme Court gets about 5,000 requests. They can choose only about 200 of these.

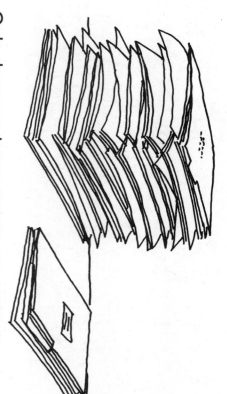

The House of Representatives

The Senate

The U.S. Senate and the U.S. House of Representatives are part of Congress. They each work in a separate part of the Capitol building.

Ⓑ

What Happens in the Capitol Building?

The Statue of Freedom stands on top of the Capitol building. It is the figure of a woman wearing a headdress of eagle feathers. She carries a sword and shield.

5

The Capitol is a symbol of the United States. When we see the Capitol, we think of our government leaders and the work that they do for our country.

7

3

The Senate wing of the Capitol has many offices and a meeting room called the Senate Chamber.

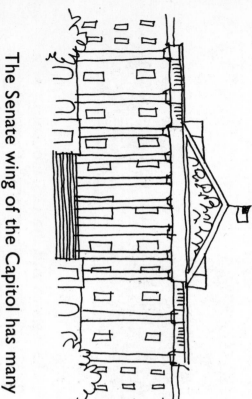

The United States Capitol is a building in Washington, D.C. It is the home of our government. Congress meets in the U.S. Capitol to make the laws of our nation.

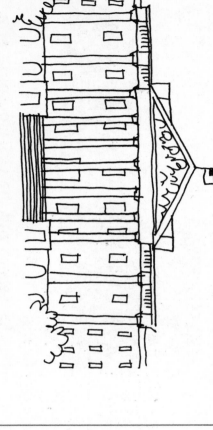

The House of Representatives wing has offices and a meeting room called the House Chamber. It also has a hall filled with statues of famous Americans.

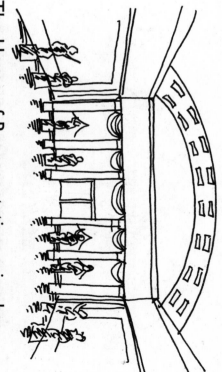

At the center of the Capitol lies the grand Rotunda. It is a large room with a high, domed ceiling. Funerals for famous U.S. citizens sometimes take place here.

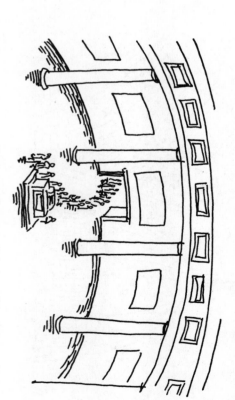

2

My state became part of the United States

in the year _____ .

It was the _____

_____ state to join the United States.

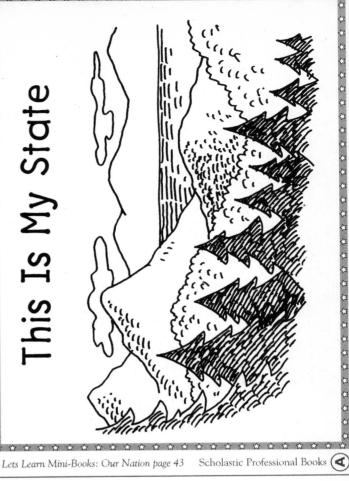

This Is My State

5

People see and do many things in my state. When visitors come, they like to

_____

_____

_____

and _____

7

I feel proud when I think about my state. What I like best about my state is

_____

_____

_____

_____

_____

1

I live in the state of
This is the shape of my state.

_____.

3

This is my state flag.
The symbols on the flag stand for

_____.

6

The capital city of my state is called

I live in the city or town called

_____.

4

These are other symbols of my state:

state bird: _____

state flower: _____

state tree: _____

This is my state song:

_____

The colonists followed English laws. They paid taxes to England. In time, the colonists grew angry. They felt that England's taxes were too high.

B

2

What Is the Declaration of Independence?

Thomas Jefferson wrote that all people deserve to have freedom and happiness. He said that a nation's government should help people to have these things.

5

Important leaders from each colony signed the Declaration because they agreed with what it said. They signed it on July 4, 1776. That day became the birthday of the United States of America!

7

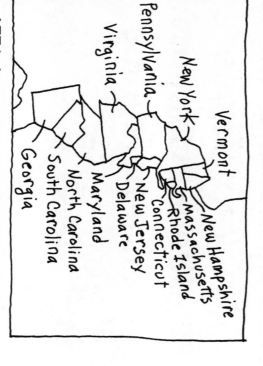

In 1776, America was not yet a country. It was a group of 13 colonies. They were ruled by a country named England.

1

The colonists decided to form their own country. They sent an important letter to the King of England. The letter was called the Declaration of Independence.

3

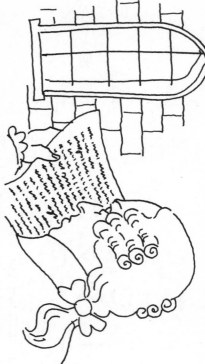

Five Americans worked together to write the Declaration of Independence. Thomas Jefferson wrote most of it. The others shared their ideas.

4

The colonists felt that England did not give them freedom or happiness. In the Declaration, they said they were breaking free and forming a new country.

6

What Does the Constitution Mean to Me?

Laws of Maryland
Laws of Vermont
Laws of New Jersey
Laws of Pennsylvania
Laws of New York
Laws of Massachusetts
Laws of Connecticut
Laws of Georgia
Laws of New Hampshire
Laws of North Carolina
Laws of South Carolina
Laws of Virginia
Laws of Delaware

In 1787, America was a new country. It was not a strong country. It was made up of 13 states. Each state made its own laws and printed its own kind of money.

Ⓑ

VOTE TODAY

Their plan said that all states would have equal power. No one person would run the United States alone. People would vote and have a say in their government.

5

Congress of the United States

ARTICLES

RESOLVED

The U.S. government still works by the Constitution today. For more than 200 years, the U.S. Constitution has helped to make and keep our country strong.

7

A country cannot run properly when it works in pieces. People knew the states needed to work together. They needed one set of rules and one form of money.

3

The United States Constitution is the rule book of America. It tells how the country must run in order to stay strong.

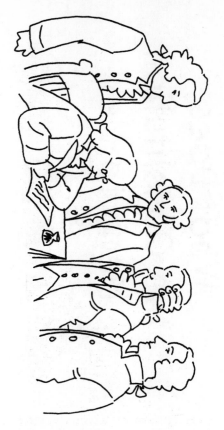

1

Fifty-five of the smartest men in America got together in Pennsylvania. They shared their ideas about government. They made a plan and wrote it down.

4

The men called the plan the United States Constitution. Every state read the plan and agreed to live by it. In 1790, the U.S. Constitution became the basis of our government.

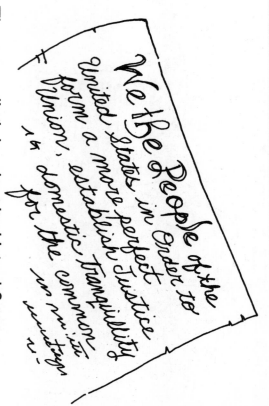

6

The Pledge of Allegiance

Most experts say Francis Bellamy wrote the Pledge in 1892. Mr. Bellamy worked for a children's magazine. He printed the Pledge in the magazine.

Ⓑ

2

On the first Columbus Day, millions of children across the United States raised the American flag over their schools. Together, they said the words of Mr. Bellamy's pledge.

5

The Pledge of Allegiance reminds Americans that we live in a country of freedom and justice. As long as we stand together, our country cannot be split apart.

7

Mr. Bellamy asked children to fly the American flag and say the Pledge. He wanted children across America to do this on one special day in 1892.

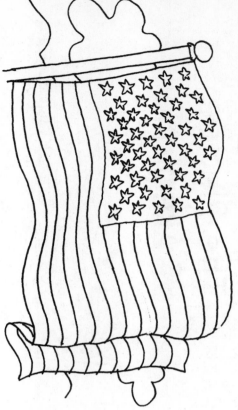

The Pledge of Allegiance is a salute to our nation's flag. It is a promise to love and be true to the United States.

That special day was the very first Columbus Day. It was a day meant to honor the discovery of America. It had been 400 years since Columbus arrived on the shores of America.

Americans still say the Pledge of Allegiance today. We promise to love and be true to the United States and to help our country however we can.

At that time, the War of 1812 was going on. America was fighting against England. One night, Francis Scott Key sat in a boat. He watched British ships fire their guns.

2

Ⓑ

The Star-Spangled Banner

Ⓐ

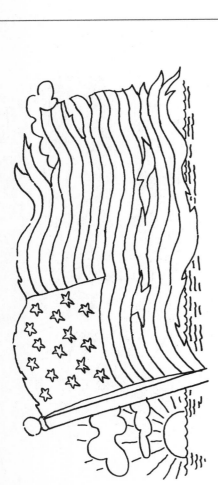

As the morning sun started to shine, the smoke lifted. Francis Scott Key could see the flag clearly now. It was red, white, and blue! America had won the battle!

5

Americans sing the anthem at ball games and other sports events. They play it on national holidays. We feel proud when we hear "The Star-Spangled Banner."

7

3

The British were shooting at Fort McHenry in Maryland. Francis Scott Key could not help his country. He could only watch while it was attacked.

4

All through the night, British guns fired. By morning, the gunfire stopped. Francis looked across the water at the fort. He could not tell whose flag he saw there.

1

"The Star-Spangled Banner" is our country's national anthem. It is the song that stands for America. A man named Francis Scott Key wrote it in 1814.

6

Francis felt proud of America. He wrote a poem on the back of an envelope. His poem became famous. In 1931, Congress declared it our country's national anthem.

2

"America the Beautiful" has become
one of our nation's most treasured songs.
It speaks of the love that
Americans feel for their country.

Ⓑ

America the Beautiful

"America! America!
God shed His grace on thee,
And crown thy good with brotherhood
From sea to shining sea.

5

"America! America!
God mend thine ev'ry flaw,
Confirm thy soul in self-control,
Thy liberty in law."

7

3

As we sing, we think about the way our country looks. We remember how hard the early settlers worked to make our country strong.

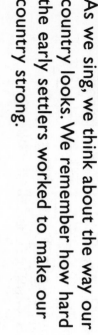

1

Long ago, a woman named Katharine Lee Bates wrote a song about the United States. She called her song "America the Beautiful."

4

Here are the lyrics:
"O beautiful for spacious skies,
For amber waves of grain,
For purple mountain majesties
Above the fruited plain.

6

"O beautiful for pilgrim feet,
Whose stern impassion'd stress
A thoroughfare for freedom beat
Across the wilderness.

The Thirteen Original Colonies

Vermont
New Hampshire
New York
Massachusetts
Rhode Island
Connecticut
New Jersey
Delaware
Maryland
Pennsylvania
Virginia
North Carolina
South Carolina
Georgia
Atlantic Ocean

Long ago, America was made up of 13 colonies. The colonies were ruled by England. They followed English laws and paid taxes to England.

B

2

The Fourth of July

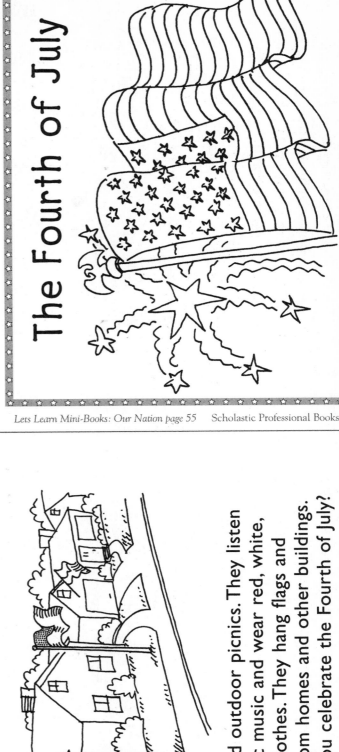

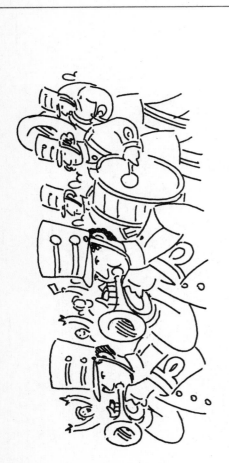

Today, we still remember what happened on July 4, 1776. We call that day the birthday of our nation. Americans have celebrated it every year since 1777.

5

People hold outdoor picnics. They listen to patriotic music and wear red, white, and blue clothes. They hang flags and banners from homes and other buildings. How do you celebrate the Fourth of July?

7

3

American colonists wanted to break free from England. On July 4, 1776, they did. On that day, American leaders signed a Declaration of Independence.

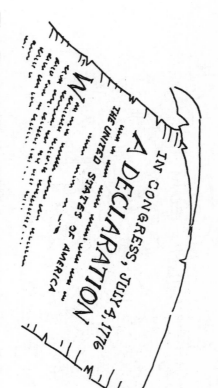

1

On the Fourth of July, we celebrate a special day. It is America's birthday.

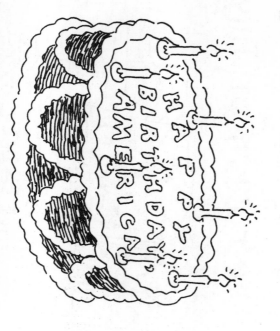

4

The Declaration of Independence said that America was going to be a free country. It would make its own laws. It would not be ruled by another country.

IN CONGRESS, JULY 4, 1776
THE UNITED STATES OF AMERICA
A DECLARATION

6

To celebrate, people hold parties across the United States. They carry flags and march in parades. They light up the skies with bonfires and fireworks.

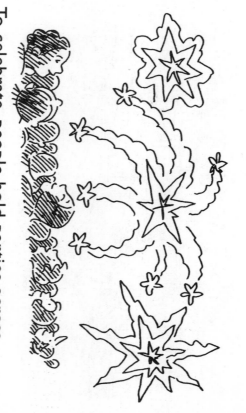

Martin Luther King, Jr., lived at a time when black Americans were treated unkindly. They were not allowed to do the same things as white Americans.

(B)

Martin Luther King, Jr., Day

Dr. King did not want people using violence to solve problems. He taught people to find peaceful ways to solve problems and seek fair treatment.

5

Martin Luther King, Jr., dreamed that someday all people would be treated as equals. In his dream, people would never again be judged by the color of their skin.

7

3

Black people and white people went to different schools. They used separate drinking fountains. They could not sit together on a bus or in a restaurant.

4

Dr. King spent his life working to change U.S. laws. He worked so that white Americans would treat black Americans fairly and as equals.

1

In January, Americans celebrate the birthday of Dr. Martin Luther King, Jr. He was a famous African American.

6

Dr. King made many speeches to teach people about equality and peace. One of his most famous speeches was about his dream for the world.

George Washington was the first United States president. People call him the "father of our country."

2

Ⓑ

Presidents' Day

Abraham Lincoln was the 16th president. He was president during the Civil War, when the Southern states wanted to form their own country.

5

THE UNITED STATES OF AMERICA

FIVE DOLLARS

We see Abraham Lincoln's picture on pennies and five-dollar bills. We remember him as one of our country's finest presidents.

7

3

George Washington made many important decisions for the United States when our country was new. He helped form the laws that still shape our nation.

4

Our nation's capital is named after George Washington. We see his picture on quarters and one-dollar bills.

1

Presidents' Day is a holiday that honors two of America's greatest presidents. They were men of courage and wisdom.

6

It was a difficult time to be president, but Abraham Lincoln was wise and strong. He stood up for his belief that America should stay together as one country.

On Memorial Day, people decorate the graves of American men and women who died in war. They place flags, wreaths, and flowers on their loved ones' graves.

2

Ⓑ

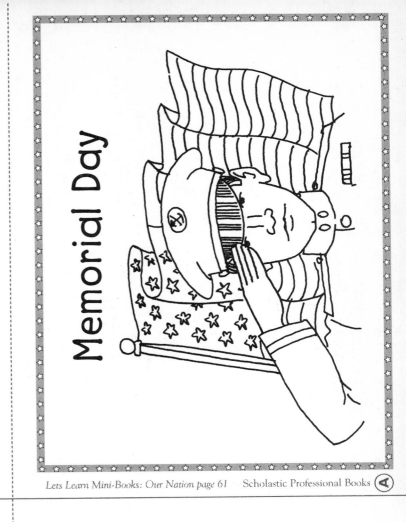

Memorial Day

Schools, banks, and post offices stay closed on Memorial Day. Some people visit with families and friends. Some gather at picnics or parties.

5

Today, it is a day to remember American soldiers from all wars. It is a chance to honor the men and women who died while protecting our country.

7

Near our nation's capital, officials place a wreath on the Tomb of the Unknown Soldier. This tomb honors soldiers who died but were not identified by name.

3

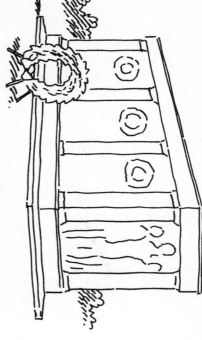

Some cities and towns hold parades on Memorial Day. Bands march and play patriotic songs. People wave flags and banners and wear red, white, and blue to match the colors in the American flag.

4

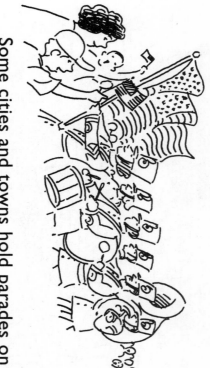

Memorial Day is a national holiday. It helps Americans remember those who died while serving our country.

1

Long ago, Memorial Day was created to remember the soldiers who died in the Civil War.

6

Veterans are people who serve in the U.S. military. They work in the Army, Air Force, Navy, Coast Guard, and Marines.

Ⓑ

Veterans Day

Veterans Day is also a time to remember veterans who have died. People visit war memorials. They decorate them with wreaths and flowers.

5

Veterans Day is a time to say thank you. It is a day to honor those who protect our freedom and help keep our nation strong.

7

3

People in the military travel the land, air, and sea to protect our nation. They work during peacetime and when our country is at war.

1

Veterans Day is a national holiday. It honors the men and women who work to protect our nation.

On Veterans Day, Americans take time to thank these brave men and women. People hold parades in their honor. They hang American flags to show thanks.

4

Many people place American flags on the graves of United States veterans. The flags let others know who served our country.

6